HABITS

THE POWER OF HABITS—
CREATING HABITS FOR SUCCESS
TO CHANGE YOUR LIFE

ADAM L. WISE

COPYRIGHT © 2015 BY ADAM L. WISE ALL RIGHTS RESERVED

This document is geared towards providing exact and reliable information in regards to the topic and issue covered. The publication is sold with the idea that the publisher is not required to render accounting, officially permitted, or otherwise, qualified services. If advice is necessary, legal or professional, a practiced individual in the profession should be ordered.

- From a Declaration of Principles which was accepted and approved equally by a Committee of the American Bar Association and a Committee of Publishers and Associations.

In no way is it legal to reproduce, duplicate, or transmit any part of this document in either electronic means or in printed format. Recording of this publication is strictly prohibited and any storage of this document is not allowed unless with written permission from the publisher. All rights reserved.

Table of Contents

Introduction 1

Chapter 1: Small Habits That Lead to a Greater Change 3

Chapter 2: Small Habits That Affect Our Journey Towards Success 9

Chapter 3: Habits That Lead to a High Level of Productivity 13

Chapter 4: How to Form a Good Habit and Make it Stick 17

Chapter 5: How to Change Your Bad Habits 25

Chapter 6: More Habits That Will Make You Successful 31

Conclusion 39

Introduction

First of all, I want to say thank you and congratulations on purchasing the book, *The Power of Habits: Creating Habits for Success to Change Your Life.*

This book contains proven steps and strategies on how to become successful by making changes in your habits that will create lasting effects.

If you feel that you have habits that are distracting you from your goals, now is the time to get rid of them and start replacing them with better habits that will lead to greater change. You can also improve your productivity by associating your habits with the right behavior. Furthermore, this book will also help you make those new habits stick.

A person's success heavily relies on that person's behavior and attitude towards one goal. By creating the right attitude towards your goal, you can develop success habits that will lead to an improved and productive life.

Motivation is also an important factor in building habits, so we have a number of examples in this book that will truly motivate and fuel you. The habit is indeed a powerful thing, and being able to truly understand it will truly change your life!

Thanks again for purchasing this book. I hope you enjoy it!

Chapter 1: Small Habits That Lead to a Greater Change

Successful people are often associated with good habits. Just by forming good habits and being goal-oriented, you, too, could have a more prosperous life. However, success doesn't come on a silver platter. Success is something that a person strives for and is brought about by passion. And since developing some strong habits will definitely lead you to a greater change in life, so here are some small habits that you can start doing to attain success:

- **Focus**: This is the very first step that you need to take before anything else. Keep yourself focused on your goal: Have a tunnel-eyed vision on that dream and never take your eyes of it. This is a small step to take and not much effort is required. If you put your mind into what you want, you are likely to get it.

- **Be Practical**: Starting a small business is one way to be successful. Although you have to be mindful of your ideas and your decisions during that time. For example, you don't have to buy an expensive license for software that you will use for your accounting or a big office if you don't have a lot of personnel. You have to be able to make a decision especially if the cheaper version of the software and a smaller office would be as useful to you as the upgraded ones. Practice frugality and properly budget your money. It doesn't hurt to watch where your money goes. Start small by listing down all that you need, take note of the things that you need vs. the things that you want. Remember that you don't have to impress anyone, but yourself alone. You can always upgrade when you have enough money.

- **Know your strengths**: Do things that you are best at, avoid getting into situations that will only get you into a rut. Utilize your talents, but still remain humble and grounded. Knowing your limits will make sure you can attain success without shooting too high.

- **Reflect**: Make it a habit to reflect at the end of every day; you'll be surprised with the new ideas and solutions that will come up. One tip is to think of three things that you are thankful about each day. Then follow it up with the things that you wish you could change. Do this every day and you may find yourself a happier person.

- **Plan ahead**: Get ahead of yourself by planning your whole day. Put the things that seem the most challenging on the top of your list. Do those things when you feel you have the most energy and are at your sharpest. Putting the less challenging things last will help you feel relaxed after finishing more difficult tasks. In short, strategically planning your day will help you become more productive.

- **Be persistent**: There will be days wherein you will experience defeat, but the most successful people have always been persistent. Persistent on achieving their goals even if they experience a problem, persistent on creating new goals to motivate them, and persistent with every setback.

- **Risk-taker**: Make it a habit to think outside the box and defy the norm. Be adventurous and be open to take on more roles. A successful person always welcomes a challenge.

- **Believe in your gut**: Sometimes you just have to stick with your gut. It is not bad to listen to your gut, they usually know better and most of the time will lead you to the right decision.

- **Make sacrifices**: If you want to be the best at what you do and succeed in everything you do, you have to be prepared to put in more hours, more effort and make all kinds of sacrifices. Always put in the extra mile, there is no such thing as an overnight success.

These seemingly small changes in your daily life will help you towards a greater and successful life over time.

Chapter 2:
Small Habits That Affect Our Journey Towards Success

Feeling incomplete? Well, the reason for that may be behind the little or small bad habits that you are unconsciously doing. You may think that these "little" habits have no effect on your journey to success, but in reality, they do. So, here are the "little" habits that we have to stop doing now:

- **Skipping breakfast**: There's a reason why breakfast is the most important meal of the day. Breakfast is the first meal you take that jump starts your day. However, skipping it deprives you of the opportunity to refuel your body. It is found out that the food taken in during the dinner from the previous day would be totally used up by your body from your heart's normal blood pumping functions and proper oxygen flow during sleep. With all of this happening while you're asleep, your body needs to be refueled upon breakfast, not only to replenish the lost nutrients during your sleep, but also to provide stamina throughout the day. The best breakfast choices include whole-grain foods matched with eggs and a fruit smoothie of your choice.

- **Constantly resorting on junk foods**: From the term itself, junk food is definitely "junk." Junk food contains little or no nutritional value and is high either in salt, sugar, fat or calories. Resorting to junk foods could cause a rise in your body's blood sugar levels since most of these foods contain a high glycemic index. Therefore, saying "no" to these foods will greatly contribute maintenance for a healthy lifestyle.

- **Drinking less water than what is recommended**: Our body contains about 60% water and health experts recommend that we should drink at least eight glasses of water every day. But don't overdrink; it *can* also cause health problems. This is because our body constantly sweats to release the waste materials and heat out from our body. Thus, failure to replenish the water in your body will cause dehydration, constipation, kidney stone accumulation and high risk of cancer, especially in the gall bladder and colon.

- **Heavy reliance on caffeine throughout the day**: A good dose of three cups of coffee in a day has its share of benefits, as researchers have revealed. However, excessive caffeine intake can disturb your sleeping cycle and cause insomnia. This is because caffeine prevents production of adenosine, which is responsible in making you feel sleepy.

- **Not exercising regularly**: Normally, people who are tired from a hard day's work would skip exercise altogether. Yes, taking a good rest would indeed energize you but in reality your body needs to take time to keep itself constantly on the move. Taking hand and body stretches and brisk walks first thing in the morning or after a long day provides good blood circulation, proper heart function, good skin complexion and good bodily form.

- **Robbing your vacation time for work**: Checking your email and squeezing in a "little" work during your vacation time is not going to be good for you. You are not allowing yourself to take the necessary break to refresh your mind and have a clearer prospective once you go back to work. Taking little breaks, like a vacation, is a healthy way to rejuvenate your body and mind.

Chapter 3:
Habits That Lead to a High Level of Productivity

Habits root themselves back from a chain reaction that starts in your brain. When your mind acquires a new learning, unless received, it is automatically incorporated in your attitude. Your attitude then commands your thoughts and then those thoughts are converted into words. Words become your actions and your subsequent actions will determine your habits. For instance, a habit of productivity comes with a decision to become productive. Being productive on a daily basis will result into a successful life.

The following are some habits of a productive person in which you can develop for a successful career:

- **Identify when you are most productive:** There is a particular time frame that a person can be at his most productive state and it differs from one person to another. This is the time in which a person allows himself to establish a more focused and highly intentional attitude towards the tasks assigned to him. As for some people, they are most productive during early mornings and early afternoon. Some people also avoid doing anything two hours prior lunchtime and dinner time, because they will feel pressured to finish everything before taking a meal. Find what's right for you and you can find yourself being more efficient and competent.

- **Utilize message filters**: Due to the tons of information generated in the Internet nowadays, updates in your email could be overflowing. Using message filters are going to be helpful in removing unnecessary messages in your inbox and filtering emails that are relevant in accomplishing your tasks. If you are a food blogger, generate your own personal filtering system that enables your inbox to filter messages relating to food, recipes and the like. There are specific message filter settings available in your respective inbox to activate this.

- **Start delegating tasks to others**: Learn to delegate your tasks. There are members of your team that can perform a particular task better than you can. Therefore it is important for you to identify the strengths and weaknesses of each member of your team. This is also the best opportunity to exercise your leadership abilities since you will develop trust and confidence with your teammates. At the same time, this gives them a shot to shine in a field they are good at. Like how the famous saying goes, "Two (or more) heads are better than one."

- **Avoid eating lunch at your desk**: If you think that eating lunch alone at your desk will make you extra productive, think again. This only deprives you of the break that you so badly need. It also doesn't help build a good relationship with your colleagues. It is okay to take a break from work; this gives you enough time to refresh your head which can help you get a new perspective and be more productive, but remember to enjoy the company of those around you.

- **Take a walk**: Go for a hike. Go to the park. Go anywhere. We all need that white space to get our creative juices flowing. So, when you feel exhausted and burned out, just relax and take a walk.

Developing a mindset and a habit of productivity is very helpful in maintaining a time and cost-efficient manner of living. One who aspires to have a successful and prosperous life must strive to make it a habit to become a productive person.

Chapter 4: How to Form a Good Habit and Make it Stick

"The greatest day in your life and mine is when we take responsibility for our attitudes. That's the day we truly grow up."

These are words from John Maxwell, a well-known inspirational speaker and leadership advocate. Taking responsibility of our attitudes and thoughts can make us more effective, productive and fruitful individuals. Good habit formation takes time and can be hard to establish. In reality, our everyday life is bombarded with different kinds of distractions that will try to divert our focus and attention away from our goals. Distractions will definitely delay us in forming and establishing good habits.

If you are one of the people who are poor in maintaining good habits, here are some tips to help you form those habits:

- **Set small goals and big goals**: All great things come from small beginnings. While having big dreams can be a good motivation, it can be really overwhelming. That is the reason you need to start small. According to a research study relating to motivation, experts have found out that conceptualized thinking (or abstract thinking) was proven to be an effective method to help with discipline. Basically, what these experts are saying is that "dreaming big" is actually helpful advice.

    A number of studies on self-determination show that creating intrinsic motivators (internal motivators that are not triggered through punishments and rewards) is an important part in creating habits that stick. What you can do is create a set of small goals or "micro-quotas" which you will have to achieve on a daily basis. These micro-quotas will contribute to the realization of your big goals or "macro-goals." Every achievement of your quota will eventually make your "big dreams" become reality.

A writer named Nathan Barry has proven that this method of forming a new habit is effective. He had started a case study in which he subjected himself to write 1000 words a day (micro-quotas) in which resulted in three self-published best-sellers and thousands of dollars for him (macro-goals).

- **Link a new habit with your existing one**: This is, by far, one of the easiest ways to form a new habit that will stick. This basically means that you are going to incorporate a new habit into your existing routine, rather than trying to overhaul your entire routine just to create a new one.

  Once you've decided on a new habit, think of creative ways on how you can integrate that to your current or existing routine. One way you can do this is by creating an "if-then" scenario to make use of an existing routine to trigger your new habit. For example, if you brush your teeth, then you have to floss. Brushing your teeth would act as a trigger to your new habit, which is flossing.

This has proven to be successful compared to forcing yourself to learn a new habit. Studies have proven that this has been helpful to make a new habit stick.

- **Removing too many options**: According to research, Steve Jobs, Mark Zuckerberg and Albert Einstein all have one thing in common. Do you know what that is? They all dress the same way every day. Steve Jobs had a dozen of those turtlenecks; Albert Einstein owned seven suits that were all the same; and Mark Zuckerberg owns a ton of grey shirts that he wears over jeans. You may be wondering what the reason behind this is. Well, they need to cut down not so important options in favor of some major decisions (why do you think they became so successful in their fields?). They believed that there are more important things to think about rather than taking the time to think of what to pull out of the closet.

Notions of these great men were proven by scientific studies on self-control. It is said that making a number of choices uses up of a lot of mental energy, even if those choices are pleasurable. So, in order to maintain long-term discipline, one must routinize what they consider the mundane choices in their life, such as choosing what to wear. The fewer the choices, the more effective you can be at developing good habits.

- **Visualize:** Humans are naturally built-in with the faculty of imagination. We have the capacity to view things as if they were physically present. Most people would start fantasizing about a new habit without really knowing the reason they want to make that change. It may be a small detail, but it's an essential part in keeping us motivated. This is the reason why experts suggest that a person fantasize about the result rather than the habit.

According to a study from UCLA, the error lies in what a person visualizes. Researchers came to a conclusion that people who are more focused on visualizing the steps that needs to be done to achieve the goal (fantasizing about learning Spanish by visualizing themselves practicing every lunch break) are more likely to succeed compared to their peers (visualizing speaking Spanish on a trip to Mexico). Visualization worked because of two reasons:

1. Planning: Visualizing helps an individual focus on the steps to achieve a certain goal.
2. Emotion: Visualization of the process reduces a person's anxiety.

- **Stop your "What the hell?" attitude:** The most obvious reason why people tend to fail at creating a new habit or making a new habit stick is because people are prone to weakness. Therefore, we tend to abandon the new habit once we slip-up.

   The best way to handle this kind of failure is to re-examine your new habit that you want to create and look for areas where you could possibly slip-up. Let's say you have problems going to the gym on a regular basis, but you tend to slip-up. When you analyzed what could be causing this, you found out that you feel lazy to get up during the morning because it's easier to just stay in bed rather than walking all the way over to the closet. What you can do to solve this is by preparing your gym clothes before you go to bed so that when you wake up and roll over you'd have the clothes ready without the need to walk over to the closet.

Forming good habits are very ideal, but it takes time, effort, dedication and commitment to cement these habits into our lives. But, with these techniques, I know that you'll be able to achieve form and start your new habits easily.

Chapter 5:
How to Change Your Bad Habits

Don't feel bad, we all have them. Bad habits are behaviors that we wish to change, but we feel that it's something that's too impossible to be done. This kind of thinking hinders us from making changes in our lives. Maybe you're thinking of finally quitting smoking. Maybe you're thinking of starting to eat healthy and ditch the junk foods. Maybe you want to even start going to the gym on a regular basis. However, right now you haven't been successful in breaking your bad habits and you're getting frustrated.

Don't be too hard on yourself. Habits are hard to break, that's the reason they are called habits. They are an important part of our everyday lives. If we didn't have any habits, we would have to think constantly about everything we do. Our habits kick in at a particular stimulus which makes us act automatically without any thinking.

From the moment you wake up and get in the shower, on your way to work where you have a habit of following traffic rules, as you go through your day and as you end your day again back to your home, you were basically running on autopilot most of the time because of your habits. This frees up a considerable amount of space in your mind and allows you to make a decision for far more important matters. Sadly, the brain cannot distinguish if a certain habit is either good or bad. Once a habit is learned, it is automatically triggered by a specific stimulus. This is the exact reason why it takes a lot of effort to change a bad habit.

But believe me, bad habits can be broken and here are 6 ways that you can break them:

1. **Figure out the underlying cause**: There is a reason why you have this certain particular habit and you have to figure out how you developed it. For example, the reason you brush your teeth is because you want to prevent having any cavities. The reason you check your email is to organize your work for the day. Those are all good habits with

positive functions. However, bad habits aren't different, and they, too, have a function.

Smoking may be your way to pass time. Compulsive eating can be your way to comfort yourself when you're feeling down. Browsing the Internet may be your way to avoid interaction from your spouse. Drinking too much liquor may be your way to deal with your family problems. If you wish to break those bad habits, you have to deal with the underlying cause.

2. **Deal with your problems**: Some people deal with problems in different ways. For instance, a workaholic would avoid eating during lunch breaks because they have a problem with leaving an unfinished task. It is clear that they have a problem and they can deal with it by seeing a professional therapist or forcing themselves to take a 15-minute break every now and then.

Even if you are aware of your problem, it isn't likely that you will stop it. So instead of stopping this habit, it is best that you replace it with a positive behavior. Positive can mean a pleasant experience, like bringing a packed lunch to the office and squeezing in a tiny 15-minute break from your busy schedule, or positive can also mean an unpleasant experience, like going to a therapy session to talk to a professional about your problem.

3. **Write it on piece of paper**: This may sound cheesy in a way, but writing your commitment on paper is the best way to make it more real. Studies show that when people write down their promises or commitments on a piece of paper and look at them at least once a day, it can help them get back on track. It's as easy as writing "I will stop smoking because I want to live long enough to see my grandchildren." Write down your commitment and look at it before you go to bed or before you even commit the bad habit and see how it will make you feel right after.

4. **Get a recovery buddy**: There is a reason why most recovery programs are held in a group

or usually use a buddy system. It just feels so much better to be able to talk to someone about your problem without being judged.

This buddy could also refer to a therapist that you go and see on a weekly basis. You can also provide support to other people in this way. The support system goes two ways, which can greatly help you maintain focus on your goal. Your buddy or counselor should be able to help you think of a positive way to deal with your bad habits.

5. **Give enough time for yourself**: Some people say that it will only take you 28 days to shake off a bad habit, but that is certainly inaccurate. Current research shows that it actually takes you around three months to completely remove a bad habit and replace it with a positive one. Bad or good habits are behaviors that are locked in the "automatic" part of your brain. They are behaviors that are going to be hard to shake off because these behaviors usually go unnoticed.

However 28 days is a good place to start in removing or altering your bad habits. Some people need a bit more time and some people need to find a gentler alternative to be able to stick to their new habits. All of this boils down to your personality, your stress level, and the support you have.

6. **Accept your slip-ups**: Do not feel discouraged whenever you slip. Take this chance to acknowledge what kinds of stimuli make you do your bad habits. You're only human, but do not give up and learn from it. This may be a clear sign that your strategy isn't working for you. Get back on track and remember that tomorrow is another day.

Chapter 6:
More Habits That Will Make You Successful

We are done talking about changing and forming new habits. In this chapter, we'll be focusing more about the different habits that you can start doing today to become highly successful in your life, career, and your relationship with others. These are habits that you can carry along as you grow older that will definitely change your life forever. This will be a pivotal point in your life and you have the chance to really change your life if you make these changes now.

Some people say that motivation is the only thing that makes you stick to a habit, but that is not entirely true. Motivation should be coupled with action which will lead into a life-changing habit that will definitely make you successful. All of the successful people in the world have an overflowing passion for what they do, but passion without hard work is nothing. If you fill your everyday lives with habits that lead you to success, you'll eventually see yourself in a position that you have dreamed of, a position wherein you are free to do anything you want and earn the money you want.

Here's a definite step-by-step guide for your guaranteed success:

1. Success is not measured by money. It should be measured by your level of happiness.

Your success should not be determined by how much you earn or what you are earning. This will only put you in a position of chasing money rather than chasing your success. Success should be seen as a journey, rather than a destination. You should start seeing your success in the same level as how you would see your happiness.

2. Read before work.

If you want to get all those creative juices flowing, try reading a good book or even just an article on your way to work. This will help you develop your creativity and increase your knowledge. Try doing this every day for at least 30 minutes.

3. Constantly wake up at the same time every day.

Develop a sleeping routine. Your body needs to recognize what times you would be active and what times you would be asleep. This will provide you more energy for the day.

4. Do your to-do list.

Get in the habit of finishing whatever you started. If you practice this in anything that you do, success is bound to find you.

5. Keep a small and easy to-do list.

Don't make your to-do list too complicated. List down a couple of the most important things you need to attend to first. Complete those before proceeding to other items on your list.

6. Keep a journal for planning and for work.

Write down ideas and thoughts. Writing down things makes them more realistic and more plausible. An idea, goal, or to-do list that isn't written down is most likely not going to happen.

7. Measurements are important.

Measure everything that you do. Every achievement that you want should be measured. This will allow you to plan carefully and have a draft on how you will attain the given goal.

8. Follow a 90-minute work plan.

Most people aren't really into being productive for the whole day. What you can do is follow a 90-minute work plan where you only focus on work for the whole 90 minutes, without checking your Facebook, Twitter, Instagram, etc. Take a break after 90 minutes and then repeat the process. This will ensure a productive work day.

9. Wake up early.

This isn't new. Most people have heard of this, but actually haven't done anything about it. Get up early in the morning every day so you can get a head start on your dream.

10. Family should be first on your list.

Family could be your significant other or your friends. Avoid working just for monetary gains. Work for a greater purpose because this is the only way to achieve true success.

11. Work harder than anyone else.

You will have competition. If you work harder than them, you will definitely gain success. Let your competition fuel you up and get you moving.

12. Create a board.

Put up a board as a reminder of all of your dreams, goals and ideas. Make sure to put it somewhere you'll always see.

13. Talk to others about your dreams.

Talk to people who share the same interest. Dream with them and talk to them about how you plan to achieve that dream, no matter how extravagant the plan is. Napoleon Hill called this relationship "a mastermind."

14. Surround yourself with "successful" people.

Only associate yourself with people who are goal-driven. Avoid being with people who are toxic and have bad influences. They will shift you away from your goals. They are not worth your time and will only slow you down.

15. Eat healthy, be healthy.

Work out. Run. Walk. Lift weights. Eat right. Get your blood pumping. Remember, a healthy body is a healthy mind.

16. Spend money on things that REALLY matter.

Luxurious things, like a flashy sports car or a classy new watch, will get you an impressive lifestyle, but not a successful one. Spend money, instead, on things that will improve your career.

17. Review those journals.

Remember those journals you made? Review them monthly so that you can stay on track and check if you are still on the right path towards your goals.

18. At the end of the day, write down 3 things you're thankful for.

This is the simplest recipe to success. Remain positive and grounded. Write down 3 things that you are thankful for every day, three things that have made an impact on your life that day. It is obvious that happy and grateful people are more likely to be successful compared to their pessimistic and sad peers.

19. Believe that you will succeed.

Believe that you can attain the goals you've set for yourself. There is no use doubting yourself because it will only hinder you from achieving your true potential. Have faith that you will be successful and, eventually, you will be.

20. Accept and learn from your mistakes.

It's cliché, but believe me, it works. Accept your mistakes and admit that you are only human. Understand that part of becoming human is screwing things up sometimes. This is the only way for you to learn effectively and gain experiences that can help you succeed in life.

Conclusion

By now you've learned the importance of habit formation, what it entails to develop new ones, and how to change an existing habit. It will definitely require a lot of hard work, but in the end, it will surely pay off. I hope that this book has also made you realize the importance of changing your habits to coincide with your goals and your dreams, and that it takes a lot of effort to really turn your habits around and lead you to success in your life, career and relationships.

Habits are extremely useful for a person and it would be impossible to run our lives without them. They are automatic responses to a given stimuli, and they free up our mind so that we can focus on other things that requires a higher form of concentration. Let's say if we have to think about chewing whenever we chew gum, or what foot to put forward whenever we walk, this would take up a lot of mental ability and we wouldn't be left with any space to perform any other function. We have a lot habits that have been deeply ingrained in our system, such as tying your shoe lace, brushing your teeth, and even breathing.

Always remember that good habits are there to create order and to create a routine which will lead to efficiency. However, bad habits can put us into negative situations and can potentially damage our well-being (i.e. smoking and gambling).

I hope this book has consciously helped you to get to know yourself better and get you to realize the bad habits that you are presently doing. It's about time to get rid of them and replace them with good habits to help you succeed and become a better person!

Finally, if you enjoyed this book, then I'd like to ask you for a favor: would you be kind enough to leave a review for this book? It'd be greatly appreciated!

Thank you and good luck!

Other books by Adam L. Wise

Crystals
Crystal Healing and Crystal Magic for Health, Love and Money

If you want to learn ancient healing and magical secrets, you should learn how to use crystals for multiple purposes in order to obtain any desired result in your life. Consult this book and you will find the answers to each and every query you have.

Feng Shui Secrets
The Ultimate Guide to Improve Your Health, Wealth and Relationships

Feng shui will be your helping hand for your health, wealth and relationships. True feng shui is no longer a mystery; it is simple and un-demanding. It is not just about planning gigantic buildings and momentous architecture. It is as simple as setting your living room in a positive and helpful way. Just give this book a read and you will be convinced of the miracles feng shui can do for you!

Erectile Dysfunction Cure
How to Naturally Cure Erectile Dysfunction Forever

There are no better means to treat a condition like this except doing so naturally. No need to experience pain, no gadgets to insert in your member, and no need to pay excessive physician fees. These all-natural treatments are not only effective, but they have become easy and discreet. Nobody will know you are getting treatment for the problem except you.

www.ingramcontent.com/pod-product-compliance
Lightning Source LLC
Chambersburg PA
CBHW061228180526
45170CB00003B/1211